D1252286

Animals
That Help Us

Horses

Jean Coppendale

QEB Publishing

Library of Congress Control Number: 2006038432

ISBN 978-1-59566-366-5

Written by Jean Coppendale
Designed by Melissa Alaverdy
Editor Paul Manning

Publisher Steve Evans
Creative Director Zeta Davies
Senior Editor Hannah Ray

Picture credits
Key: t=top, b=bottom, l=left, r=right, c=center, FC=front cover
Alamy: p. 7 tr View Stock; p. 13 ct Günter Gollnick; p. 14 bl
Adrian Sherratt; p. 20 cl The Geoff Williamson Image Collection.
Corbis: contents page Tom Brakefield; p. 4 bl Thierry Charlier/
Sygma; p. 4–5 Lindsay Hebberd; p. 6–7 David Stoecklein; p. 8–9
Dan Lamont; p. 9 cb Elder Neville/Sygma; p. 14–15 Ron Watts;
p. 18–19 Graham Tim/Sygma; p. 19 tr Tim Thompson; p. 20–21
Larry McDougal; p. 22–23 Steve Chenn. Getty Images: p. 10
Graham Robertson/Reportage; p. 12–13 Johner/Johner Images.
©RDA: title page, p. 16–17, p17 tl. Rex Features: p. 10–11:
JB/Keystone USA.

Printed and bound in China

Words in **bold** can be found in the Glossary on page 23.

Contents

How horses help us

Horses help us in many ways. They work on farms, in forests, and on busy city streets. Some horses are specially trained to help disabled children learn how to ride. Horses also take part in parades and entertain us at shows. Different types of horses do different jobs.

These horses are helping fishermen catch shrimp off the coast of Belgium, in Europe.

Rodeo riders lead a parade through the streets of Dallas, Texas.

Horses on land

Horses have worked on land for hundreds of years. Today, machines do a lot of the work that horses used to do. But on **ranches**, horses are still used to round up **cattle** and rescue cows that have strayed from the rest of the herd.

A **cowboy** uses a **lasso** to round up runaway cattle.

In parts of Scotland, farmers still round up sheep on horseback.

Horsepower!

In forests and woodlands, strong horses are often used to pull heavy loads, instead of tractors. This is because people enjoy working with horses, and horses do not do as much damage to the land.

When trees have been chopped down, horses drag the logs through the forest to the road. Then, the logs are loaded onto trucks.

A tug on the reins will give this powerful working horse the signal to start pulling its heavy load.

On this Christmas tree farm in the United Kingdom, two horses work together to pull a trailer.

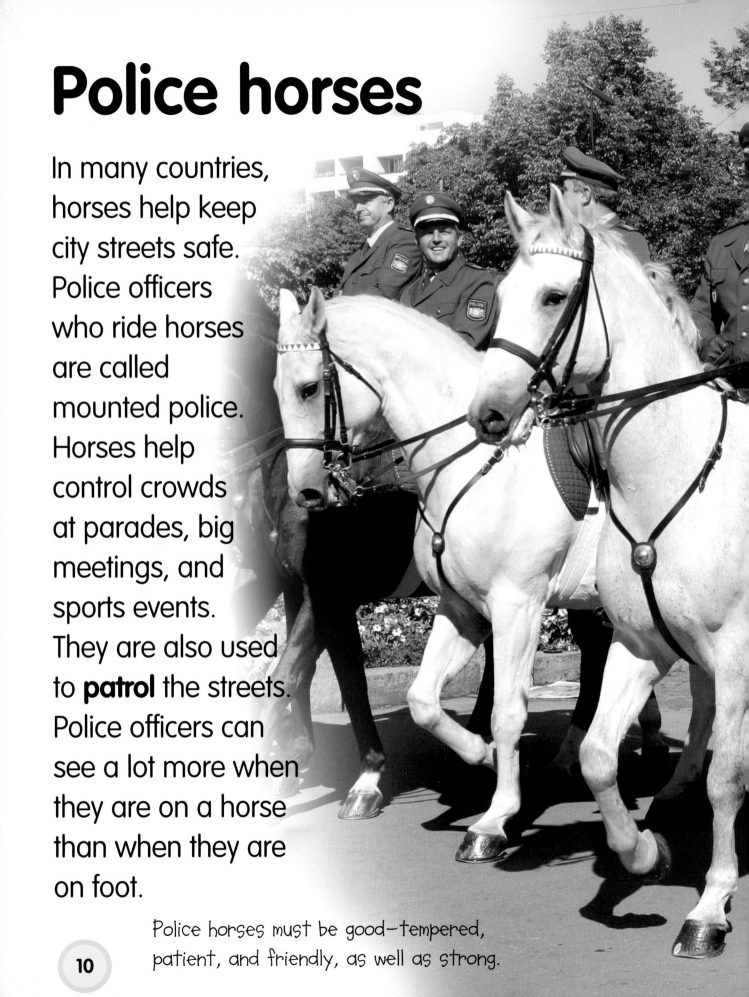

Police horses

In many countries, horses help keep city streets safe. Police officers who ride horses are called mounted police. Horses help control crowds at parades, big meetings, and sports events. They are also used to **patrol** the streets. Police officers can see a lot more when they are on a horse than when they are on foot.

Police horses must be good-tempered, patient, and friendly, as well as strong.

Police horses and their riders sometimes wear face guards for protection.

Wedding horses

In some countries, beautiful horses take the bride to the ceremony in a white carriage. Sometimes the horses wear **garlands** of flowers, bells, and other brightly colored decorations. After the wedding ceremony, the horses and carriage take the bride and **groom** to the reception.

White horses are often chosen to pull wedding carriages. The correct term for a "white" horse is a "gray."

In this picture, a groom on a decorated pony leads a wedding procession through the streets of India.

Vacation horses

Horses can make vacations more special. In some big cities, visitors can hire a horse and buggy for a **sightseeing** tour.

Many people also enjoy riding in the country or **trekking** on horseback through beautiful countryside. Riding a horse is much healthier and more fun than riding in a car!

Riding is a great way to make friends and explore new places.

The horses enjoy the fresh air and exercise, too.

A tour in a horse-drawn carriage is even more exciting in the snow!

Horses for learning

At some riding schools, specially trained horses are used to teach disabled children to ride. Many of the children go on to take part in special events and competitions for disabled riders.

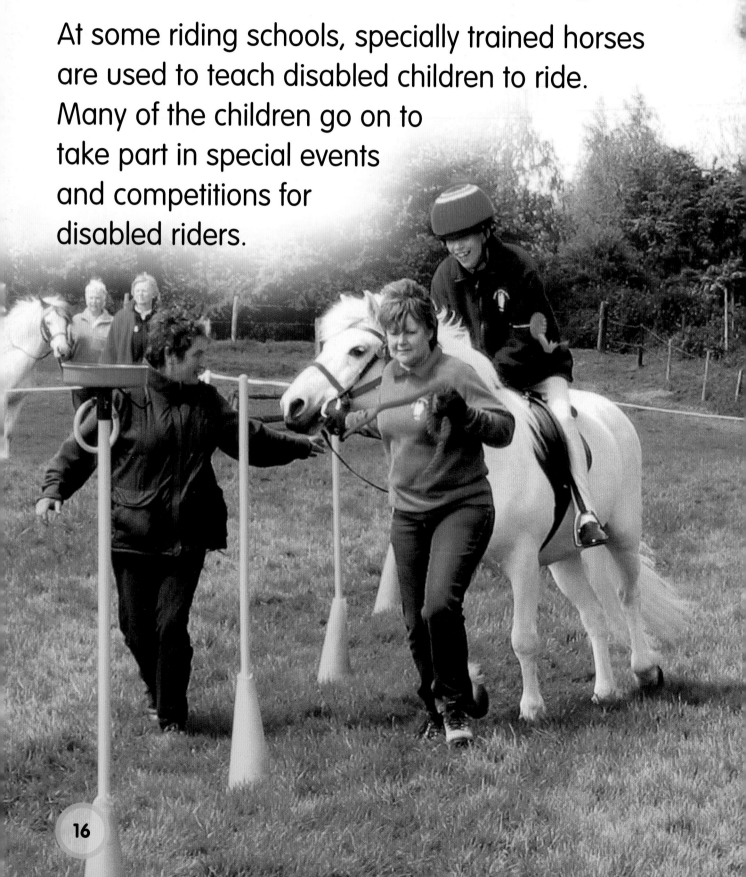

These ponies know they must be gentle with their riders. There are plenty of helpers to keep the children safe.

The children become very close to the ponies and love the challenge of learning new skills.

Horses on parade

In London, in the United Kingdom, huge crowds gather every year for the Trooping of the Color. This is a grand display to mark the Queen's birthday. Military bands and soldiers on horseback parade past Buckingham Palace, where the Queen lives.

In Canada, the Royal Canadian Mounted Police (the "Mounties") put on a special display every year. The riders and their horses perform to music and end with an exciting **gallop**.

More than 200 horses take part in the Trooping of the Color.

The Mounties' musical ride is a test of skill for both the horses and their riders.

Show horses

Horses take part in many different shows and events all over the world. In the United Kingdom, a gymkhana is a riding competition which is often organized by the local pony club. Events include jumping, **dressage**, and races.

In show jumping, a rider who jumps all the fences successfully scores a "clear round."

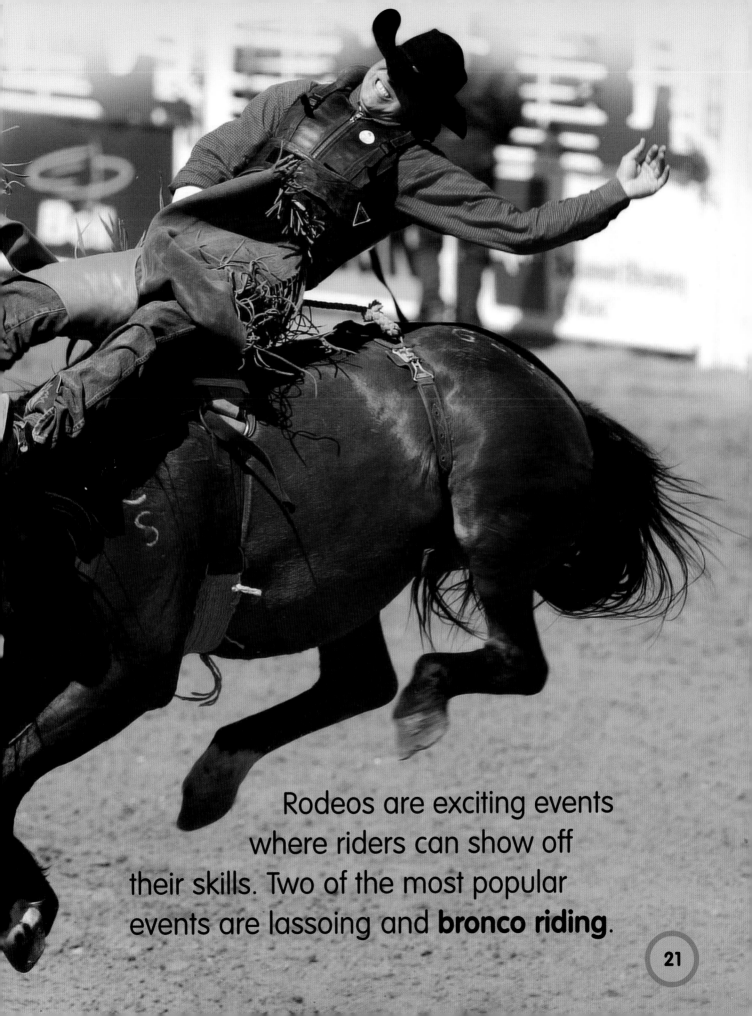

Rodeos are exciting events where riders can show off their skills. Two of the most popular events are lassoing and **bronco riding**.

Activities

- Imagine you are one of the horses from this book. Which horse would you like to be? Why? Make up a story about your day as this horse and draw a picture.

- What sort of work do you think the horse in this picture would do?

- Make a picture of a horse. Collect scraps of material for its coat, pieces of wool or string for its mane (the thick hair on the back of its neck), and shiny paper for its hooves.

- Make a horse scrapbook. Collect pictures of horses from magazines and newspapers and paste them into a sketchbook. Make notes about what the different horses do. Try to include as many different types of horse as possible, from police horses to Indian wedding horses.

Glossary

bronco riding
riding a wild or partly trained horse without a saddle

cattle
a group or herd of cows

cowboy
a farm or ranch worker

dressage
a set of movements that test a rider's skill and control over their horse

gallop
a fast horseback ride; the fastest a horse can go

garland
a necklace woven from flowers

groom
a man who has just been married or is about to be married

lasso
a length of rope with a loop at one end, used to catch cattle

patrol
to walk or ride around an area to make sure everything is safe

ranch
a farm where cattle or horses are reared

rodeo
a popular event in which cowboys show off their riding skills

sightseeing
visiting special places of interest

trekking
traveling on horseback through mountains, desert, or countryside

Index